Girlology

RELATIONSHIPS WHIZ

Facts and figures about families, friends and feelings

Elizabeth Raum

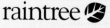

raintree

a Capstone company — publishers for children

Raintree is an imprint of Capstone Global Library Limited, a company incorporated in England and Wales having its registered office at 264 Banbury Road, Oxford, OX2 7DY - Registered company number: 6695582

www.raintree.co.uk myorders@raintree.co.uk

Text © 2018 Capstone Global Library Limited 2018
The moral rights of the proprietor have been asserted.

Edited by Mandy Robbins
Designed by Kayla Rossow and Charmaine Whitman
Original illustrations © Capstone Global Library Limited 2018
Picture research by Jo Miller and Kelli Lageson
Production by Kathy McColley
Originated by Capstone Global Library Ltd Printed and bound in India

ISBN 978 1 4747 4811 7
22 21 20 19 18
10 9 8 7 6 5 4 3 2 1

British Library Cataloguing in Publication Data
A full catalogue record for this book is available from the British Library.

Acknowledgements
We would like to thank the following for permission to reproduce photographs:
Shutterstock: 3355m, 30b, AstroStar, 25t, Brocreative, 8, Eric Isselee, 12b, ESTUDI M6, 11b, fotoinfot, 26, Franz Pfluegl, 10r, HagenProduction, 13t, Ilenoleum, 5, Jaren Jai Wicklund, 9t, Kwanbenz, 12t, Larysa Ray, 10l, Layland Masuda, 7, Ljupco Smokovski, 31b, Lopolo, 17r, Lucky Business, 11tl, mainfu, 31m, Maja K, cover-l, Maridav, 28, Mila Supinskaya Glashchenko, 14, mohd farid, 30r, Monkey Business Images, 24, 9b, 9m, Nowick Sylwia, cover-r, Oaurea, 4, oneinchpunch, 29t, Patryk Kosmider, 11tr, Petra's Vectors, 25l, PhotoMediaGroup, 23, Rawpixel.com, 17l, 19, Robert Kneschke, 25b, sirtravelalot, 27, Suwat Sirivutcharungchit, 13b, Syda Productions, 16, VGstockstudio, 29b, wavebreakmedia, 20, 22, 31t, WAYHOME studio, 15

Design Elements
Capstone Studio: Karon Dubke; Shutterstock: AD Hunter, Alemon cz, Angie Makes, Antun Hirsman, chyworks, Gizele, Petra's Vectors, RedKoala, Sonya illustration, TairA, Undrey

Printed and bound in India.

CONTENTS

Chapter 1

SHARING JEANS AND GENES

Who are you closest to? Is it your family, your friends or maybe even your pet? Your very first relationships are with members of your family. How have these relationships shaped who you are? You may share interests and values with your family.

You may even share clothes with a brother or sister. But how close are you biologically? Genes define the traits or characteristics you have inherited from your parents. Do you want to know how many genes you share with members of your family?

PERCENTAGE OF GENES SHARED ON YOUR FAMILY TREE

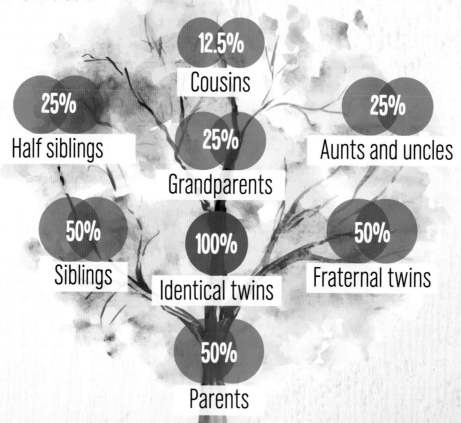

12.5%
Cousins

25%
Half siblings

25%
Grandparents

25%
Aunts and uncles

50%
Siblings

100%
Identical twins

50%
Fraternal twins

50%
Parents

FAMILIES TODAY

There is no one way to define a family. Some, such as adoptive or foster families, don't share any genes. It's not all about biology. It's about a group of people who are committed to each other and their well-being.

31.3% — Nuclear family: 31.3% of children are the biological children of two married parents living together.

27% — Single-parent family: In 27% of families, either a mum or dad is responsible for bringing up the children.

20% — Blended family: At least 20% of families include members from two or more previous families, such as step-parents, stepbrothers and stepsisters.

10% — Multi-race family: 10% of children live in families where the members are of different races.

6.3% — Extended family: 6.3% of grandparents take on the role of parents to their grandchildren.

Around **4,500** children are adopted every year in the UK.

In the UK, around 20,000 dependent children live in same-sex couple families.

PARENTS: A SOMETIMES TRICKY RELATIONSHIP

Whether you live with biological parents, step-parents, adoptive parents or others, the adults in your life play a major role. They can be a great source of support as you grow up.

Relationships between parents and children often change between the age ranges of 8 to 11 years and 12 to 14 years. As you get older, you feel more independent. You want to make your own decisions. Sometimes these changes make the relationship between children and parents more difficult.

How does your relationship with your parents compare with that of other children your age? In 2016, Time for Kids and KidsHealth.org surveyed 9,000 children aged between 8 and 14 to ask if they agreed with the following statements. This is what they discovered:

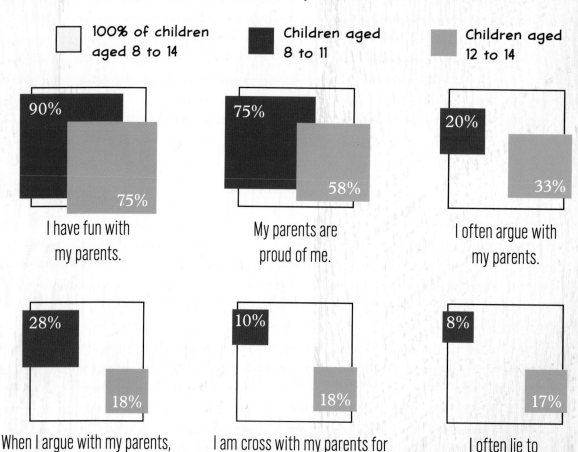

100% of children aged 8 to 14

Children aged 8 to 11

Children aged 12 to 14

90% / **75%** — I have fun with my parents.

75% / **58%** — My parents are proud of me.

20% / **33%** — I often argue with my parents.

28% / **18%** — When I argue with my parents, we make up quickly.

10% / **18%** — I am cross with my parents for a long time if they upset me.

8% / **17%** — I often lie to my parents.

WHO DO TEENAGERS TALK TO?

Teenagers don't always feel comfortable talking to their parents. Who do you talk to about what's going on in your life? It may depend on the issue. A survey posted on StatisticsBrain.com in 2016 asked teenagers who they talk to about various topics.

Talks to:

Father   Mother   Friends   No Answer

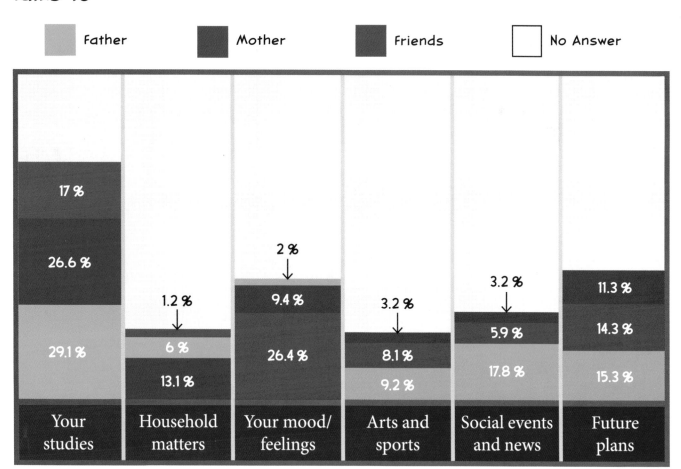

| Your studies | Household matters | Your mood/ feelings | Arts and sports | Social events and news | Future plans |

Conversation topic

BIRTH ORDER:
WHERE YOU FIT IN YOUR FAMILY

Did you know that your position in a family may affect your personality? Scientists have studied birth order and its effect on people for decades. They've found some interesting personality trends in oldest, middle, youngest and only children. Whether it's because of your relationship to your siblings, the way your parents treat you, or another factor, birth order does seem to matter.

First-borns are often natural leaders. They also tend to have higher IQs than their younger siblings.

reliable

organized

successful

perfectionist

First-born

leader

confident

serious

conservative

ambitious

FUTURE TIP: Married couples who have different birth orders tend to have the most successful, long-lasting relationships.

empathetic
relaxed
negotiator
independent
middle child
social
creative
loyal
patient

Middle children are usually great negotiators, which could mean they'd be successful politicians. Perhaps that's why **52%** of American presidents have been middle children.

rebellious
performer
outgoing
funny
carefree
last-born
creative
charming
affectionate

Youngest children are most likely to start their own business. According to a British study of 6,300 people, **49%** of youngest children were likely to become their own boss by the age of 38.

successful
logical
confident
perfectionist
ambitious
only child
creative
studious
well-spoken
particular

Only children tend to share a lot of traits with first-borns. Because they spend so much time with adults, they often act like "little adults".

1/2 of British families now contain only one child.

TWINS! A UNIQUE RELATIONSHIP

Identical twins are the closest blood relatives possible. They share 100% of the same genes. Does that mean they behave the same, like the same foods and choose the same fashions? Probably not. After all, it's their appearance that's identical, not their personalities. Researchers have studied both identical and fraternal twins for decades. Some of their discoveries may surprise you.

DID YOU KNOW...

Identical twins do not have identical fingerprints.

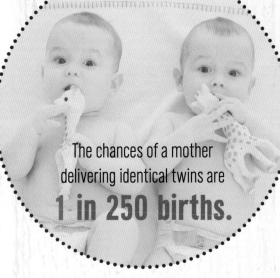

The chances of a mother delivering identical twins are **1 in 250 births.**

For women taking fertility drugs, the odds of having twins is **1 in 38 births.** These are usually fraternal twins, but not always.

A woman's chance of having identical twins increases between 2 to 8 times when she's on fertility drugs.

Twins interact in the womb. They have a relationship even before they are born!

If you are an identical twin, your chance of giving birth to twins is no greater than anyone else's. However, if you are a fraternal twin, you have a **1 in 17** chance of having twins.

The chances of a mother delivering fraternal twins are

3 or 4 in 250 births.

40%
of twins invent their own language.

Chapter 2

FURRY FRIENDS

In families with pets, the pet often plays an important role, bringing happiness and comfort in good times and bad. So, how do teens compare to the rest of the population when it comes to pets? 67% of teens prefer dogs to cats. What other kinds of animals are popular pets with teenagers?

TEENAGERS' PET PREFERENCES

In 2015, the website stageoflife.com surveyed teenagers about their preferred pets.

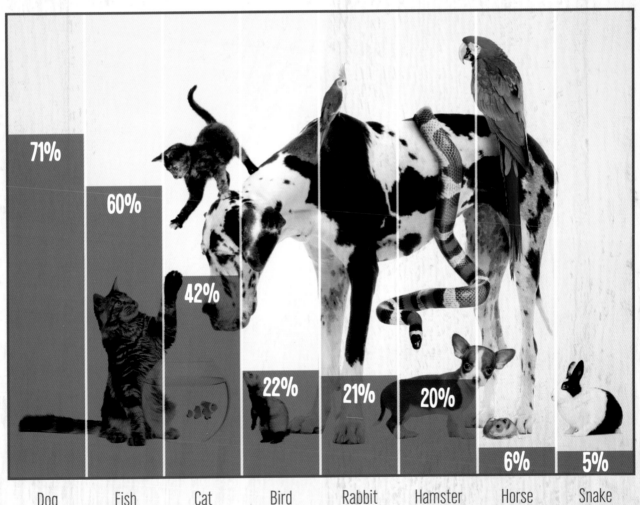

Dog	Fish	Cat	Bird	Rabbit	Hamster	Horse	Snake
71%	60%	42%	22%	21%	20%	6%	5%

HEALTH BENEFITS OF OWNING PETS

Pets provide benefits beyond their unconditional love and support. Did you know that having a relationship with a pet is good for your health? A 2016 survey of pet owners showed that many recognise these health benefits:

Health benefit

Improve physical and mental well-being		71%
Reduce stress		88%
Reduce depression		86%
Reduce anxiety		84%
Improve heart health	60%	
Help with memory	56%	
Help in classroom learning	45%	
Prevent childhood allergies	32%	

Owners who knew

NON-PET OWNERS

Only 7% of teenagers have never owned a pet. Why?

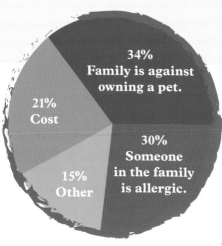

34% Family is against owning a pet.

21% Cost

30% Someone in the family is allergic.

15% Other

Chapter 3

YOUR CIRCLE OF FRIENDS

Other than family, our closest relationships are often with friends. Unlike family, you can choose your friends! Some friends have known each since they were very young. Friendships change as we grow older, but they remain one of our strongest relationships.

FRIENDSHIPS DEEPEN WITH AGE.

Age	What friendship can mean
3–6	Friends are local children who like to do the same things. Each child wants his or her own way. Friendships come and go, often ending in fights.
5–9	A friend is someone who does nice things for you, such as saving a seat or sharing a treat. This is the age when having friendships becomes very important.
7–12	Friends play by the rules. They share and cooperate. Children judge friends harshly if they are not kind or don't meet one another's expectations of what a friend should do.
12 +	Mature friendships develop. Friends feel emotionally close to one another. They accept and value differences, and understand if a friend wants to spend time with others. Friends trust one another and remain close even during long separations.

FRIENDSHIP FACTOIDS

Friends can help us live longer! Having a strong friendship circle increases your chances of living longer by **50%**.

Friends affect our success. Working with a friend who is more capable than you makes you **10%** more productive. On the flip side, working with a friend who is less capable than you makes you **10%** less productive.

Friends can affect our health. People with strong friendships tend to overcome illness better than those without them. However, friends can also lead us into unhealthy habits such as smoking and overeating.

We're drawn towards people similar to us. Studies have shown that people share more genes with friends than with strangers.

83% of teenagers say that their best school memories revolve around friends.

41.8% of teenagers say they experienced their greatest moments of joy with friends.

HOW BIG IS YOUR CIRCLE OF FRIENDS?

Several studies have asked these questions: How many friends do most people have? How many of our friends are "real" friends?

During your lifetime, you are likely to make **396 friendships.**

A total of **33** are lasting friendships.

Of these, only **6** will be close friends.

The other **27** will be more casual friends.

DUNBAR'S NUMBER

British researcher Robert Dunbar studied communities throughout history to determine the number of friends people had in various times and cultures. Recent studies have supported his findings about layers of friendship at any one time. Think about your social circle. Does Dunbar's Number reflect your friendship circle?

Closest friends:
5

Good friends:
10

Secondary friends:
35

Third-layer friends:
100

Friendship tips

Follow these tips in order to make the most out of your friendships:

- Don't rush it. Lasting friendships develop slowly over time.

- Listen to what your friends are saying and ask appropriate questions.

- Don't seem needy. Someone who craves attention is a huge turnoff.

- Give compliments, whether it's something they're wearing or something they've done.

- Be helpful. Offer assistance and do favours for your friends without expecting payback.

- Be trustworthy. Don't gossip or reveal secrets that friends share with you.

DIGITAL FRIENDS

Computers and mobile phones allow us stay in touch with friends or make friends in new ways. Can you think of some ways that online friendships are different from in-person friendships?

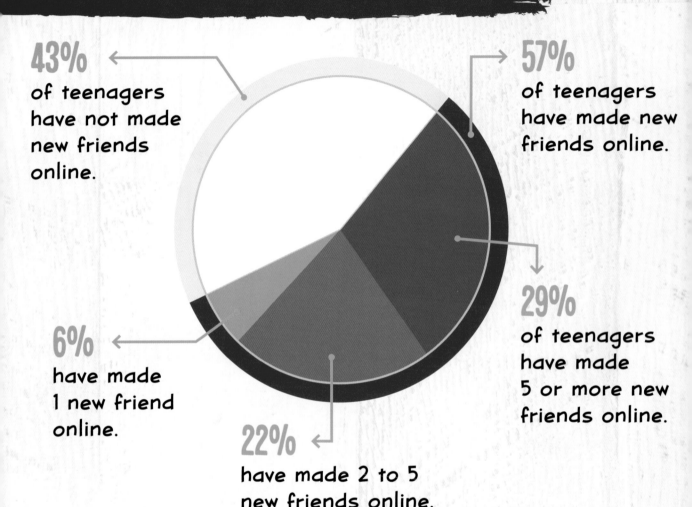

43% of teenagers have not made new friends online.

57% of teenagers have made new friends online.

29% of teenagers have made 5 or more new friends online.

6% have made 1 new friend online.

22% have made 2 to 5 new friends online.

MEETING IN PERSON

It's one thing to make new friends online. It's another to meet them in person. There's no way to know if a friend you've met online is actually who they say they are. How many teenagers have met an online friend in person?

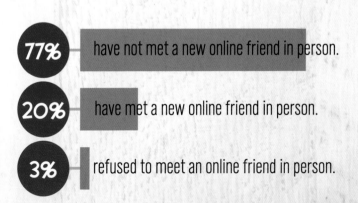

77% have not met a new online friend in person.

20% have met a new online friend in person.

3% refused to meet an online friend in person.

STAYING IN TOUCH DIGITALLY

Digital media hasn't just opened the door to meeting new friends. It's a great way to stay in touch with all your friends when you're not together. According to a 2015 Pew Research Center Survey, US teenagers report that, on a daily basis:

 **70%** text their boyfriend or girlfriend more than they talk on the phone.

 **12%** spend more time connecting with their boyfriend or girlfriend on social media than in person.

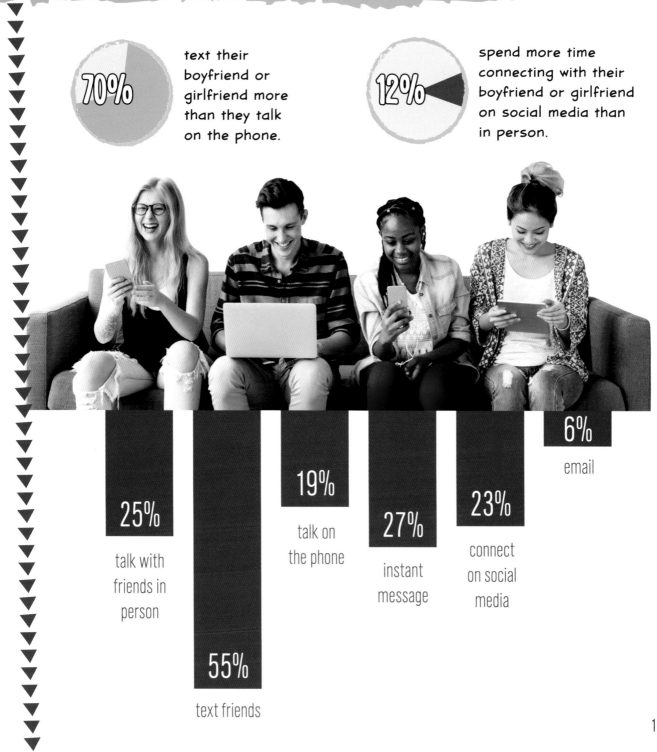

25% talk with friends in person

55% text friends

19% talk on the phone

27% instant message

23% connect on social media

6% email

TOXIC FRIENDSHIPS

No one wants to lose a friend, but sometimes friendships become toxic. That's when you need to walk away.

Unhealthy friendships can actually make YOU unhealthy. A study undertaken at the University of California, in the US, found that toxic friendships cause high levels of stress. High stress levels cause inflammation in your body. The inflammation can lead to diabetes, heart disease and even cancer.

A toxic friendship is one in which you are consistently being mistreated. This could be emotional or physical abuse. Toxic friendships bring out the worst in people. So how do you know if you're in a toxic friendship?

TOP 5 SIGNS YOUR FRIENDSHIP IS TOXIC

1 Unpleasant behaviour

Someone who mistreats you or others is not a friend.
This could be verbal abuse or even physical abuse.
Anyone who treats you in a way that makes you feel unhappy
is someone you shouldn't spend time with.

2 Gossip

Someone who talks about others in nasty or unkind
ways may be gossiping about you, too.

3 Neediness

Someone who needs your attention constantly, but is rarely
there when you need him or her, is not a good friend.

4 Selfishness

Someone who only cares about her own interests and
ignores yours is not a true friend. She may make you feel
left out or pressure you to do things you don't want to do.

5 Conflict

Constant disagreements can put too much stress on
a frienship. A stressful friendship isn't good for your health.

BEING BULLIED

Some bullying situations start with toxic friendships. Sometimes classmates, neighbours or even strangers act like bullies. Even brothers, sisters or friends can act like bullies, too. What types of actions qualify as bullying?

TYPES OF BULLYING

Verbal   teasing, name-calling, taunting, threatening to cause harm, inappropriate sexual comments

Social   spreading rumours, leaving someone out, embarrassing someone in public, telling others not to be friends with a particular person

Physical   hitting, kicking, pinching, spitting, tripping, pushing, breaking someone's things, making rude gestures

TIP: If you are bullied, find supoprt. Speak to a kind friend or trusted adult. Bullies shy way from people who have a support system.

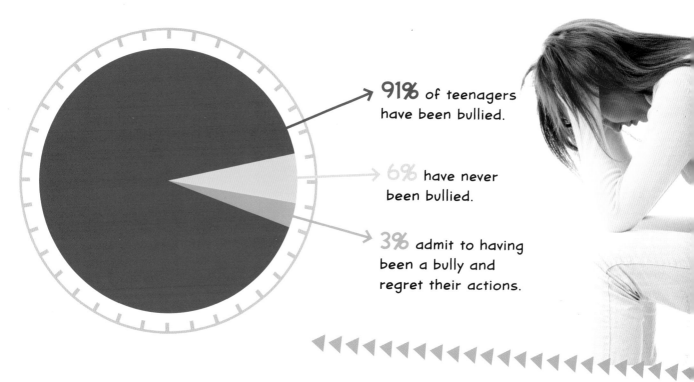

91% of teenagers have been bullied.

6% have never been bullied.

3% admit to having been a bully and regret their actions.

TOP REASONS TEENAGERS SAY THEY HAVE BEEN BULLIED

- **23%** looks or size
- **19%** being clever or "geeky"
- **13%** interests or hobbies
- **9%** race
- **6%** being poor
- **4%** having a physical or learning disability
- **2%** being rich
- **2%** sexual orientation

Chapter 4

ROMANCE IN THE AIR

By the age of 12 or 13, many children have developed crushes. A crush describes intense feelings you may develop towards another person. There are different kinds of crushes. All of them are perfectly normal.

Have you ever had a crush? If so, what type?

IDENTITY CRUSH

An identity crush describes intense admiration for someone who you would like to be more like. You admire a person's good characteristics. It might be a teacher, sports coach, older pupil at school, a neighbour, a friend or even a family member.

CELEBRITY CRUSH

Sometimes you can feel a strong connection to and admiration for actors, actresses, musicians and sports stars. Chances are you'll never meet your favourite celebrity. But you may put up posters, buy films or music, and keep up with the latest celebrity news.

ROMANTIC CRUSH

You feel intensely drawn to a person romantically. You may daydream about the person or even flirt. But when you're a pre-teen, chances are you don't have much actual contact with this person.

LOVE AND FRIENDSHIP

Love and friendship may seem very different, but when asked, teenagers often look for the same qualities in a boyfriend or girlfriend that they do in a friend. What do you think of these answers? Would you agree or disagree?

MOST IMPORTANT FACTORS IN A LASTING ROMANTIC RELATIONSHIP

Girls say:

		Boys say:
Honesty/trust	**1**	Honesty/trust
Friendship	**2**	Similar values and morals
Mutual respect	**3**	Similar interests
Similar values and morals	**4**	Physical attraction

LOVE AND LOSS

How does love affect other relationships? Teenagers report that falling in love may change your circle of friends. Unfortunately, that sometimes means losing friends.

51% of girls have been "dumped" by a friend in favour of spending time with a boyfriend.

32% of boys have been "dumped" by a friend in favour of spending time with a girlfriend.

18% of teens admit that having a girlfriend or boyfriend has had a negative impact on a relationship with a close friend.

Chapter 5

HEALTHY RELATIONSHIPS

Whether the relationship is with family members, friends, boyfriends or girlfriends, you need your relationships to be healthy. But what does that mean? A healthy relationship is one in which you feel valued and respected. It's a connection to another person that makes you a better person for having it. And while every friendship, couple and family has their ups and downs, all healthy relationships have certain features in common:

Trust and honesty
A healthy relationship of any kind requires honesty. If you can't trust someone, you can't truly connect.

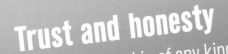

Support
In both good and bad times, healthy relationships provide encouragement and compassion.

Individuality

In a healthy relationship you'll feel free to be yourself. You'll also accept the other person for who they are.

Fairness

A healthy relationship has a give-and-take quality. You take turns making decisions and compromise.

Mutual respect

The people involved value and understand one another.

Great communication

You can talk to one another and express your feelings and opinions freely.

HEALTH, HAPPINESS AND FRIENDSHIP

The best relationships are not only fun, they also promote good health and happiness. Experts report that good relationships can be lifesavers! There's even a course at the University of California in the US called The Science of Happiness. The basis of the course is that supportive, healthy relationships are very important to well-being.

DID YOU KNOW...

Having a friend who is happy can boost your happiness by **15%**.

An unhappy friend can reduce your happiness by **7%**.

A study of 10 year olds in the Netherlands showed that **having friends reduces stress.**

An Australian study found that children who have good social relationships tend to be happier as adults.

People with stronger social relationships have a

50%

greater chance of surviving to old age than those with weaker social relationships.

Author bio

Elizabeth Raum is a full-time writer who has lived in 12 different cities and towns in the US. She currently lives in Fargo, North Dakota, USA. Her favourite ways to stay in touch with friends and family are face-to-face visits, email, talking on the phone, texting and social media. She is fascinated by statistics and hopes you are too.

Books in this series:

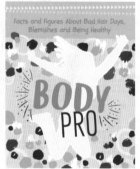
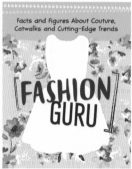

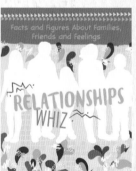